# The Messiah in the Appointed Times

by Donald McCluskey

Illustrated by Kate Orr



– Second Edition 2026 –



www.TheAppointedTimes.com

www.AncientWords.us

# Contents

# Reading and Viewing Schedule

Ancient Words traveled to the land of Israel to create a collection of videos to accompany the lessons in this guidebook. The purpose of the videos is to provide additional information about the Appointed Times and to connect the concepts of *The Messiah in the Appointed Times* to the land where the spring Appointed Times were fulfilled by Jesus, some 2,000 years ago.

The videos are free to view and may be accessed by scanning the QR code below or by navigating to the URL in your browser.

The dates for reading and viewing are provided for those who wish to honor the Messiah in the Appointed Times on (or near) the actual dates on the Jewish calendar. Of course, they may be studied and viewed at any time of year as you seek to learn more about the Messiah in the Appointed Times. Enjoy!

# Navigate to:

**www.TheAppointedTimes.com/calendar**

Or scan the QR code below:

## Introduction to
# The Messiah in the Appointed Times

The Appointed Times, also known as the Jewish holy days, were established in the Law of Moses almost 3,500 years ago.[1] These sacred events were given by the Lord for the people of Israel to honor and observe every year on specific dates throughout each year—four in the springtime and three in the fall—as festivals, new moons, and Sabbath days.[2] They were given to Israel to annually teach about their Messiah, who would be Jesus of Nazareth, making them as relevant to Christians as they are to the nation of Israel.

The Appointed Times that occur in the springtime commemorate the founding of Israel as a nation,[3] including their exodus from Egypt, their perilous journey into the wilderness, the crossing of the sea, and their meeting the Lord at Mount Sinai when He gave His Law to the people.

But of far greater importance, the Appointed Times foreshadow significant events in the Messiah's redemptive work. The *spring* Appointed Times are shadows of His first coming, 2,000 years ago — teaching of His death, burial, resurrection, and giving the Holy Spirit—clearly identifying Jesus of Nazareth as the promised Messiah.

The *fall* Appointed Times foreshadow the return of the Messiah[4] on the Day of Trumpets, including ascending His glorious throne, the resurrection of the dead, reward, and judgement. The Day of Atonement gives insight into how the Messiah obtained eternal redemption, and the Feast of Booths holds the idea of the Messiah taking up residence in the heavenly Jerusalem with His redeemed.

The purpose of this booklet is to present a brief explanation of each Appointed Time on the left-hand pages and the Messiah's fulfillment on the right-hand pages. Our prayer is that your faith will be strengthened as these words reinforce that Jesus is truly the Lord's Messiah, our hope of glory.

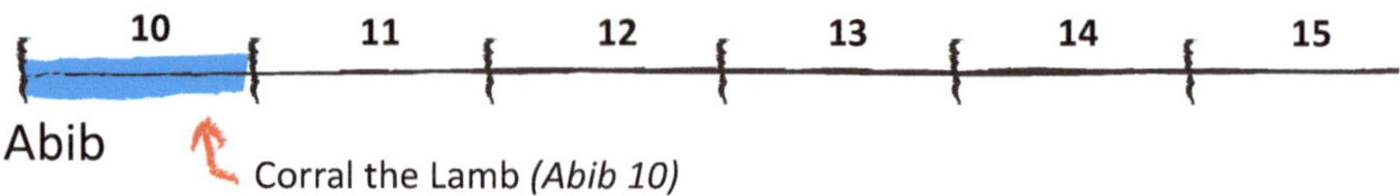


## Testing the Purity of the Lamb

Immediately after the ninth plague, the plague of darkness, the Lord told Moses to "**Speak to all the congregation of Israel, saying, 'On the <u>tenth of this month</u> they are each one to take a lamb for themselves, according to their fathers' households, a lamb for each household.**"[5]

What was the reason for taking a lamb and isolating it? According to the Talmud,[6] the lamb was set apart for the purpose of inspecting it or testing it for its purity and worthiness to be the Passover sacrifice.[7] The Passover lamb was to be observed from the 10th day of the month through the 14th day.[8] Moses taught that sacrifices must be perfect to be accepted; there shall be no defect in it,[9] which was the reason for the inspection.

Why did the Passover sacrifice have to be perfect to be accepted? We learn from the Lord's words, many years later, when He rebuked the people, saying, "But when you present the blind for sacrifice, is it not evil? And when you present the lame and sick, is it not evil? Why not offer it to your governor? Would he be pleased with you? Or would he receive you kindly?"[10]

In the same way, it was absolutely necessary that the Passover sacrifice was unblemished and spotless before it was presented to the Lord, or else it would not be accepted and would not accomplish the objective of shielding the worshipper from the peril that was to come.

# Testing the Purity of the Lamb of God

All four gospels, Matthew, Mark, Luke, and John, record Jesus' Triumphal Entry into Jerusalem[11] - a key Messianic event. In doing so, Jesus presented Himself to the nation of Israel as the Lord's Passover Lamb. This event also took place on the **tenth day of the first month**[12] and later became known as Palm Sunday. It is not a coincidence that it was the exact date that Israel corralled their Passover lambs to observe them for their purity.

But how could the Messiah, the Lamb of God, be tested for purity? Certainly not in the same way as the Passover lambs were tested, but the 22nd chapter of Matthew records a series of tests that the Jewish leadership posed to Jesus – questions about His righteousness and adherence to God's Word.[13] Through His responses, He demonstrated His own purity as the Passover Lamb of God.

Jesus' responses to the interrogations were perfect, silencing His rivals. The end result is recorded in Matthew 22:46: **"No one was able to answer Him a word, nor did anyone dare from that day on to ask Him another question."** Indeed, the Lamb of God was found to be without spot or blemish.[14]

But Jesus was not finished proving His worthiness, so He posed a question to His interrogators. Referring to Psalm 110:1, He asked them "If David then calls Him 'Lord,' how then is He his son?" [15] In other words, how could a son be greater than his father? The answer? **David's son is the Messiah**, and as He told the woman at the well, "**I who speak to you am He.**" [16] In these words, **Jesus not only demonstrated His purity, but His pedigree as the Son of God.**[17]

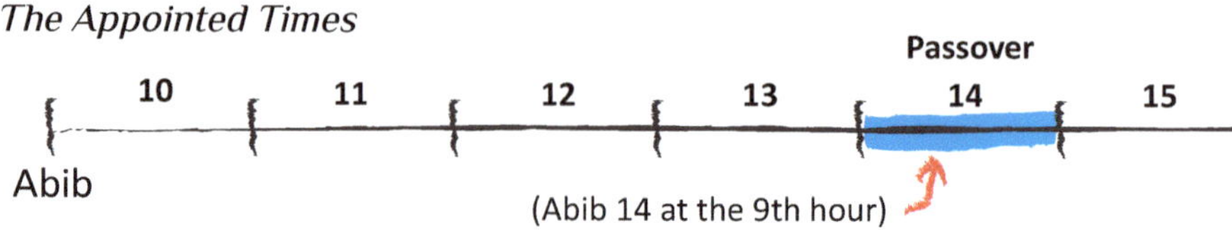


## Passover – Sacrifice the Lamb

The Lord continued His instructions to Moses in the 12th chapter of Exodus, saying, "**You shall keep it until the fourteenth day of the same month, then the whole assembly of the congregation of Israel is to kill it at *twilight*. Moreover, they shall take some of the blood and put it on the two doorposts and on the lintel of the houses in which they eat it.**" [18]

"**...The blood shall be a sign for you on the houses where you live; and when I see the blood I will pass over you, and no plague will befall you to destroy you when I strike the land of Egypt.**" [19]

The timing of Passover was very specific. It cast a prophetic shadow of the death of the Messiah on the fourteenth day[20] of the first month[21] at twilight. When twilight[22] is used in the writings of Moses, it most likely refers to the time between the ninth hour (3 PM) and sunset. Thus, the unblemished Passover lambs were sacrificed on the fourteenth day at the ninth hour during the year of Israel's exodus from Egypt, creating the timing shadow of the Messiah's sacrifice.[23]

The shadow of this Appointed Time is seen in the death of a spotless lamb that died so that others could live. A grave peril was visited on every home that was not covered by the blood of the lamb. Yet, an infinitely greater peril will be pronounced against every individual who is not protected by the blood of the Messiah – the Lamb of God. Do you know how the blood sacrifice of Jesus the Messiah is credited to a person?[24]

## Passover – The Sacrifice of the Lamb of God

The Apostle John tells us, "**Now it was the day of preparation for the Passover; it was about the sixth hour. And he [Pilate] said to the Jews, 'Behold, your King!' So, they cried out, 'Away with Him, away with Him, crucify Him!' ... So he then handed Him over to them to be crucified.**"[25]

Why is it significant that Jesus died on the day of preparation for the Passover?[26] It is significant because that day is **the <u>fourteenth day</u> of the first month**, the very same day that the Israelites in Egypt sacrificed their Passover lambs and displayed the blood on the doorposts and lintels.

Furthermore, the gospels of Matthew, Mark, and Luke record that Jesus breathed his last at the **<u>ninth hour</u>**,[27] which corresponds to the twilight sacrifice of the Passover lambs, between the ninth hour and sunset.

Once again, it is not a coincidence that Jesus' death coincided with the death of the Passover lamb in both the day and the hour. The Apostle Paul tells us that **Christ our Passover** has been sacrificed,[28] clearly teaching that Jesus is our Passover lamb.

Now, it becomes clear how the testing of Jesus after His Triumphal Entry was the fulfillment of testing the Passover lamb, and His crucifixion fulfilled the sacrifice of the Passover lamb. Both events fulfilled the shadows of these Appointed Times.[29]

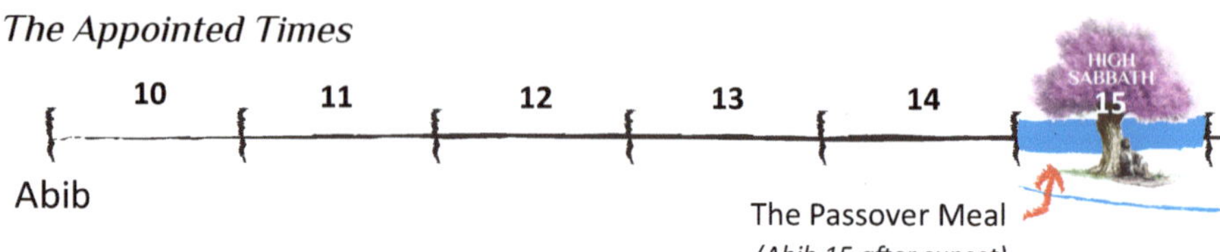


# The Passover Meal – Death, Affliction, and Bitterness

The Jewish day ends and begins at sunset.[30] When the sun set on the fourteenth day, the date changed to the fifteenth, when they were to eat the Passover lamb. The Lord said, "**They shall eat the flesh that same night, roasted with fire, and they shall eat it with unleavened bread and bitter herbs.**" [31]

What is the significance of the ingredients of the Passover meal? Moses made it very clear that unleavened bread is the ***bread of affliction***[32] because the people were leaving Egypt in haste and their dough did not have time to become leavened. Thus, the name, the *bread of affliction*.

The exodus from Egypt was truly a journey of affliction.[33] The bitter herbs depicted their fear and flight from Pharaoh, as the people and their families became trapped between his army and the sea.

Think about the imagery that is cast in the shadow of this Appointed Time: the deceased lamb, the bread of affliction, and bitter herbs. Clearly, the journey of the Israelites was a journey of affliction, but what did it foreshadow about the Messiah? Jesus endured affliction and the bitterness of death. But there is an even closer parallel that is embedded in this Appointed Time, and the answer becomes clear when we consider the timing of the Passover meal along with its substance.

Just so you know, the Passover meal was the inaugural meal of the seven-day **Feast of Unleavened Bread**.[34] For seven days, all Israelites were forbidden from eating or drinking anything that contained leaven.

# Jesus' Burial – Death, Affliction, and Bitterness

**"When evening had already come, because it was the preparation day, that is, the day before the Sabbath, Joseph of Arimathea came, a prominent member of the Council, who himself was waiting for the kingdom of God; and he gathered up courage and went in before Pilate, and asked for the body of Jesus."**[35]

When the sun set on the day of Jesus' crucifixion, the date became the fifteenth[36] of Abib,[37] the first day of the **Feast of Unleavened Bread** – the time and day when the people of Israel consumed the Passover meal. While they ate the bread of affliction, tasted the bitter herbs, and consumed the sacrificed lamb, the Lamb of God tasted the bitterness of death as He was entombed in Joseph's grave.[38]

Indeed, the mock trials and abuse at the hands of soldiers were a source of great affliction, but the cross struck swiftly and brought bitter death to the Messiah. After the sun had set, the deceased Lamb of God was laid in the tomb as His friends sought to quickly lay Him to rest as the first high Sabbath of the Feast of Unleavened Bread began.

At this point, the Messiah's journey culminated as He entered the greater and more perfect tabernacle that was not made by human hands, where He obtained eternal redemption[39] with His atoning blood for all mankind. With this victory in hand, He made proclamation to the spirits now in prison, who were once disobedient.[40] In addition to this, another great victory of the Messiah would soon be realized in the next Appointed Time: First Fruits!

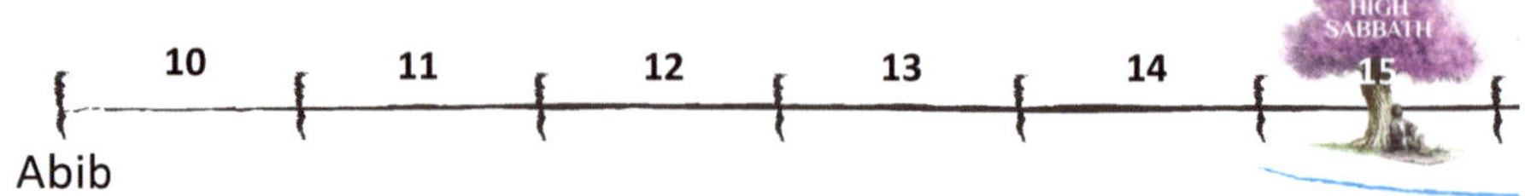

# The First Fruits Shadow

The Jewish Talmud states that "on the fourteenth day of the month of Nisan [also known as Abib] ... they killed the Passover sacrifice; **on the fifteenth they went out, and that day was Friday.**"[41] Moses tells us that the Lord brought them out of Egypt **by night**,[42] and we learn that the people camped **three times**[43] during their flight from Egypt until the miraculous passing through the sea on *the third day*.[44] He also recorded that the Israelites were safe on the other shore of the sea at *daybreak*.[45]

When we put the pieces together, it becomes clear that the Israelites rose alive from the sea at daybreak on Sunday morning, which is the very same time that the Messiah rose alive from the grave almost 1,500 years later. Both of these events occurred on the Sunday morning after the Passover meal was eaten.

Why are these details important? It is because this particular Sunday, the day after the weekly Sabbath, is the day of **First Fruits** – an Appointed Time in Leviticus 23. The first fruits were presented on the day after the *Sabbath*,[46] which is always the Sunday that occurs during the Feast of Unleavened Bread.

Could it be a coincidence that Jesus arose alive from the grave on the same day and time that Israel rose alive from the sea? Could it be a coincidence that Israel's journey of affliction began in the nighttime of the fifteenth and lasted for three nights and days, the same timing that Jesus was in the tomb? It seems absurd to suggest such a thing – it is clearly the hand of God shining a spotlight on His Messiah through the nation of Israel so the whole world could recognize Him as the Anointed One of God.

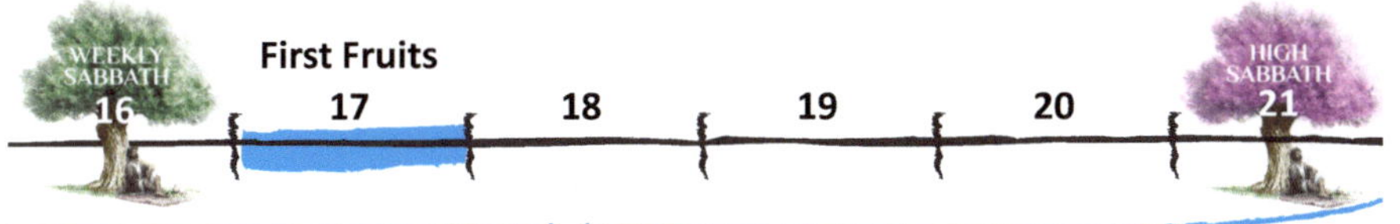


## The First Fruits of the Resurrection

Clearly, there is perfect alignment between Israel rising alive from the sea and Jesus rising alive from the grave at dawn on First Fruits. So, let's explore the meaning of *first fruits*,[47] since the meaning of the Appointed Times belongs to Christ.[48]

When the people of Israel brought their first fruits offerings to the Lord, they were bringing the first of their produce to Him with the expectation that He would bless them with additional produce. This is the essence of first fruits: a gift, acknowledging that which has already been given, accompanied by an expectation that more will come.

In the context of the resurrection of the dead, the Apostle Paul tells us, "But now Christ has been raised from the dead, the first fruits of those who are asleep."[49] Indeed, in His resurrection, Jesus is the first of many who will be raised from the dead. He is the first fruits and those who call on His name will be the fruits that follow.

A few verses later, Paul further clarifies that Jesus is the first of those who have been redeemed. "But each in his own order: Christ the first fruits, after that those who are Christ's at His coming..."[50] When we celebrate Jesus' resurrection from the dead on First Fruits, we can also celebrate the expectation and hope of our own resurrection from the dead on that great day to come![51]

Through the atoning blood of Jesus, we have eternal redemption; through His resurrection, we have the magnificent hope that we will also be raised from the dead to live with Him as immortals forever!

# The Feast of Weeks – The Meeting at Mount Sinai

The next Appointed Time is the **Feast of Weeks**, which is also known as **Pentecost**.[52] This is the day that the Israelites met the God of their fathers at Mount Sinai, when He gave them His law.[53] It was a terrifying event for the people, as they perceived the thunder and lightning flashes and the ominous sound of the ram's horn and the mountain smoking – they trembled and stood at a distance.[54] The Lord said, "You yourselves have seen that I have spoken to you from heaven."[55]

This Appointed Time commemorates the meeting with the Lord at Mount Sinai and it foreshadows a wonderful day to come. It is observed by counting fifty days[56] from the day of First Fruits. On this day, the people were to present two loaves of leavened bread to the Lord and have a special ceremonial gathering and not do any laborious work, which indicates a high Sabbath day.

What might be intimated in the shadow of this Appointed Time, with the Almighty God descending in a terrifying way and giving His law to the people? And what is pictured in the wave offering of two loaves of leavened bread?[57] If unleavened bread represents affliction,[58] is it possible that leavened bread might represent life and vitality?

These images seem contrary, but when the substance of this Appointed Time is revealed, they make perfect sense. What could be a fulfillment that would give life and vitality to people? What could reside within us as rivers of living water? Jesus said, "He who believes in Me, as the Scripture said, from his innermost being will flow rivers of living water. But this He spoke of the Spirit, whom those who believed in Him were to receive."[59]

# The Feast of Weeks – The Meeting In Jerusalem

Fifty days after Jesus rose from the grave on First Fruits, His followers were gathered together in Jerusalem. The second chapter of Acts provides clear detail about this event:

"When the **day of Pentecost** had come, they were all together in one place. And suddenly there came from heaven a noise like a violent rushing wind, and it filled the whole house where they were sitting. And there appeared to them tongues as of fire distributing themselves, and they rested on each one of them. And they were all filled with the Holy Spirit and began to speak with other tongues, as the Spirit was giving them utterance."[60]

This is the fulfillment of the ***Feast of Weeks*** Appointed Time. In this visitation, however, the Lord did not descend in a terrifying way, but rather as their ally and friend, giving them power as Jesus foretold, to be His witnesses to the remotest part of the earth.[61]

What made the difference? Why did the Lord present Himself in a terrifying way at Mount Sinai, but as an empowering ally and friend some 1,500 years later? The answer is clear. It was because of the atoning blood of Jesus the Messiah that was shed to cleanse them and make them wholly acceptable to God the Father. "He saved us, not on the basis of deeds which we have done in righteousness, but according to His mercy, by the washing of regeneration and renewing by the Holy Spirit, whom He poured out upon us richly through Jesus Christ our Savior."[62] The Holy Spirit indwells all believers in the Messiah!

## Reflecting on the Spring Appointed Times

The apostle Paul taught that the elements of the Appointed Times — the festivals, new moons, and Sabbath days — are shadows of what is to come. More importantly, however, their substance or meaning belongs to Christ.[63] Jesus of Nazareth, indeed, fulfilled the shadows of the spring Appointed Times with perfect precision in their timing and substance some 2,000 years ago, proving beyond a shadow of doubt that He is the Messiah of God.

*"Unless a grain of wheat falls into the earth and dies, it remains alone; but if it dies, it bears much fruit."*

## Anticipating the Fall Appointed Times

With this fulfillment confirmed, we now turn our attention to the fall Appointed Times to understand times and events that are still future — events of Messianic magnitude that are yet to come that will cause our planet to tremble and shake with the wrath of God and the judgments of the Messiah. In Revelation 10:7, the mighty angel declares that the mystery of God - the gospel - is finished with the sounding of the seventh trumpet, which is the first of the fall Appointed Times.

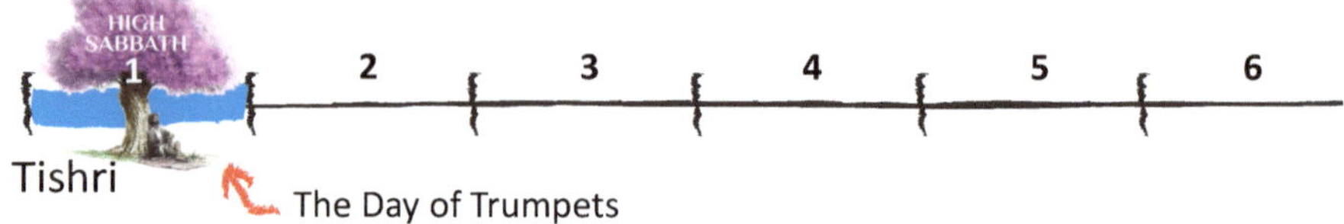

## The Day of Trumpets – Yom Teruah

The Day of Trumpets, also known as Yom Teruah, is a mysterious Appointed Time – the Lord gave very little information about the activities of this day, and almost no information about its meaning and significance. It is clear, however, that it is to be observed on the first day of the seventh month, when the silver edge moon appears in the night sky, signaling the start of the month of Tishri.[64]

It is interesting that the underlying word for this Appointed Time does not mention trumpets – the word is teruah, which refers to noise, shouts, commotion, praise, commands, etc.[65] Trumpets can certainly be part of teruah, but it can involve much more. The Lord said that this day will be a **reminder**[66] by teruah with a holy convocation and no laborious work – it is a high Sabbath day. On this day, the people raise their teruah to the Lord.

As the revelation of the Scriptures unfolded over the centuries, the Jewish people observed a strong connection between the teruah and characteristics of this Appointed Time with that which is found in Psalms 47 and 98.[67] The teruah of these psalms include the roar of the sea, rivers clapping their hands, mountains singing, people clapping hands, shouts, trumpets, singing praises, and melody with musical instruments, including lyre and horn.

What is the reason for this joyous teruah in these psalms? It is the return of the Messiah – a great king over **all the earth**, subduing nations, revealing His salvation and righteousness, **remembering** His lovingkindness and faithfulness, giving an inheritance, ascending His throne, and judging the earth and the world while His princes are assembled before Him. Can you imagine what the Messianic fulfillment might be for this Appointed Time?

## The Day of Trumpets – The Return of the Messiah

Jesus and the apostles make it very clear that the Messiah will return with the sounds of teruah – shouts, trumpets, and loud voices.[68] The events of this great day will include the return of the Lord, the resurrection of the dead, judgement and reward, and the Messiah ascending His glorious throne. This event will indeed signal the culmination of the gospel[69] and the end of the world as we know it.

"And He will send forth His angels with A GREAT TRUMPET and THEY WILL GATHER TOGETHER His elect from the four winds, from one end of the sky to the other."[70]

"For the Lord Himself will descend from heaven with a **shout**, with the **voice of the archangel** and with the **trumpet of God**, and the dead in Christ will rise first. Then we who are alive and remain will be caught up together with them in the clouds to meet the Lord in the air, and so we shall always be with the Lord."[71]

"Behold, I tell you a mystery; we will not all sleep, but we will all be changed, in a moment, in the twinkling of an eye, at the **last trumpet**; for the trumpet will sound, and the dead will be raised imperishable, and we will be changed."[72] "Then the **seventh angel sounded**; and there were **loud voices in heaven**, saying, 'The kingdom of the world has become the kingdom of our Lord and of His Christ; and He will reign forever and ever.'"[73]

Is the Day of Trumpets truly a shadow of the return of the Messiah? "Be on the alert, for you do not know which day your Lord is coming."[74]

HIGH SABBATH 1 2 3 4 5 6

Tishri

# The Day of Atonement – The Shadow

The Day of Atonement is observed on the tenth day of the seventh month[75] – it is the most solemn day in all Israel. It is on this day that the high priest entered the most holy place with the sacrificial blood to make atonement[76] for himself and his household and then make atonement for the nation of Israel. The imagery of this ceremony[77] is profound, giving insight into the atonement that the Messiah made for our sins and the sins of the whole world, some 1,500 years later.[78]

As part of the ceremony, the high priest presents two goats before the Lord at the doorway of the tent of meeting. Lots were cast to decide which will be the Lord's goat and which will be the scapegoat.[79]

The Lord's goat was sacrificed and the high priest brought its blood into the most holy place in a golden basin where he stood before the ark of the covenant. Burning incense formed a cloud of smoke above the ark where the Lord said He would meet him in the cloud.[80] It must have been terrifying to stand face to face with the Lord, protected only by the blood. At this point, he dipped his finger into the blood seven times and sprinkled it seven times before the ark to make atonement for the sons of Israel.

After this, the high priest came out of the holy place and cleansed it and the altar with the blood. He then placed his hands on the head of the scapegoat and confessed all the iniquities, sins, and transgressions of the people onto it and then released it into the wilderness to bear all their iniquities to a solitary land.[81] Do you see the Messiah in this imagery – a goat without sin, shedding its blood for forgiveness of others, and the scapegoat carrying the sin of the people far away from the presence of God?

The Day of Atonement

## The Day of Atonement – Jesus Our High Priest

The writer of the book of Hebrews tells us that the priests of the Law serve a copy and shadow of the heavenly things,[82] but Jesus has obtained a more excellent ministry, serving in the actual heavenly tabernacle.[83] The first tabernacle was a copy and pattern of heaven that was given to help us understand how He fulfilled the shadow of the Day of Atonement.

Recall that the high priest was required to make atonement for himself and his household before he could make atonement for the nation.[84] Jesus did not have to do this, since He was without sin. But in the same way the high priest entered the most holy place with innocent blood to stand face to face with God, Jesus entered the heavenly tabernacle with His own blood and stood face to face with the Almighty to make atonement for us and obtain eternal redemption.[85]

The book of Hebrews tells us, "But when Christ appeared as a high priest of the good things to come, He entered through the greater and more perfect tabernacle, not made with hands, that is to say, not of this creation; and not through the blood of goats and calves, but through His own blood, He entered the holy place once for all, having obtained eternal redemption."[86]

The shadow that is cast by the Day of Atonement is clear and the Messiah's fulfillment is crystal clear. Jesus is our high priest, and when He died on the cross, He entered the heavenly tabernacle to make atonement – forgiveness of sin – for all who would believe on Him. "Let it be known to you, brethren, that through Him forgiveness of sins is proclaimed to you, and through Him everyone who believes is freed from all things, from which you could not be freed through the Law of Moses."[87] Halleluiah, what a Savior!

## The Feast of Booths – Taking Up Residence

The final Appointed Time, the Feast of Booths, is the most festive and joyous of all. In this seven-day feast,[88] the Lord commanded the people to celebrate and rejoice – not just the heads of the households, but every native-born in Israel, including the sons, daughters, servants, priests, orphans, widows, and even strangers in town – *Have a great time and that's an order!*

The feast was an outdoor celebration, where every household was to build a festive, temporary shelter, which was called a *booth* or *sukkah*,[89] complete with table, food, and drink to celebrate the blessings of the Lord. It was a perfect time for friends, family, and neighbors to casually visit and feast and enjoy friendly times together to give thanks for the harvest. But it was also a commemoration of the journey of affliction when their ancestors lived in booths during the very difficult journey in their exodus from Egypt.[90]

It seems so strange, however, that the Lord would schedule the most joyous Appointed Time only five days after the most solemn Day of Atonement. Why would He do that?[91] The reason is that the cleansing and forgiveness of the Messiah's atoning blood was perfect and thorough, to the extent that all offenses, past, present, and future, were completely forgiven, bringing perfect peace and reconciliation between God and mankind. What greater reason for celebrating and rejoicing could there ever be?

Consider the Messianic shadow of this Appointed Time with people taking up residence with great celebration. It is interesting that, during the Feast of Booths, the Lord also took up residence in the temple that Solomon built almost 500 years after the exodus.[92] Could this Appointed Time be a shadow of the ultimate residence for the Messiah and those who believe?

19 20 21 HIGH SABBATH 22 23 24

# The Feast of Booths – The Heavenly Jerusalem

"Then I saw a new heaven and a new earth; for the first heaven and the first earth passed away, and there is no longer any sea. And I saw the holy city, new Jerusalem, coming down out of heaven from God, made ready as a bride adorned for her husband. And I heard a loud voice from the throne, saying, 'Behold, **the tabernacle of God is among men**, and He will dwell among them, and they shall be His people, and God Himself will be among them...'"[93]

After the great judgement in the 20th chapter of Revelation, the mood of the prophecy changes from apocalyptic calamity to a world of ultimate peace, with the throne of God and the Lamb[94] as the centerpiece of the magnificent heavenly Jerusalem. In this new world, on this newly created planet, we find the bride of Christ – those who are redeemed by the atoning blood of the Lamb, reigning with Christ in paradise,[95] with the river of the water of life freely flowing to nourish the immortal human frame.[96]

Is this pristine planet, the heavenly Jerusalem, the fulfillment of the shadow of the Feast of Booths?[97] Are the dwelling places in this new world the same that Jesus mentioned when He said, 'In My Father's house are many dwelling places... for I go to prepare a place for you. If I go and prepare a place for you, I will come again and receive you to Myself, that where I am, there you may be also'?"[98] I believe they are!

The Messianic fulfillment of the Feast of Booths is found on a newly created, pristine planet that hosts the throne of God and the Lamb where the redeemed serve the immortal King – and we will forever be with the Lord!

## Book References in Endnotes

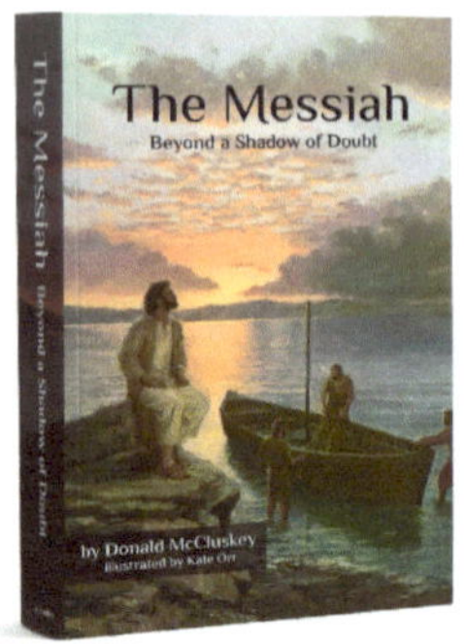


While this booklet presents a high-level overview of how the Appointed Times foreshadow the Messiah, many readers desire deeper exploration of this subject. **The endnotes below that begin with "M" refer to page numbers in The Messiah Beyond a Shadow of Doubt**, which provides additional information, detailed analysis, and documentation about the Messianic teachings of the Appointed Times.

ISBN: 978-0-9966758-7-1

## Get the Book

TheAppointedTimes.com/bookstore

## Endnotes

1. The Appointed Times are listed in chronological order in the 23rd chapter of Leviticus.
2. M9 & 17
3. M9-12
4. M14-15
5. Exodus 12:3
6. The Talmud is an authoritative body of Jewish literature that provides commentary on the Law of Moses.
7. M71
8. M70
9. Leviticus 22:21
10. Malachi 1:8
11. M123
12. M125-129
13. M130-133

14. M135
15. Matthew 22:41-45
16. John 4:26
17. M133-135
18. Exodus 12:6-7
19. Exodus 12:13
20. M72
21. Exodus 12:2 identifies the first month of the year as Abib
22. Moses used the phrase "between the two evenings," which is most often translated as twilight in modern Bibles.
23. M72
24. "As Moses lifted up the serpent in the wilderness, even so must the Son of Man be lifted up; so that whoever believes will in Him have eternal life. – John 3:14-15
25. John 19:14-16
26. M147-148
27. Matthew 27:45-50, Mark 15:33-37, Luke 23:44-46
28. 1 Corinthians 5:7
29. Colossians 2:16-17
30. M323-325
31. Exodus 12:8
32. Deuteronomy 16:3
33. M83 (Somber Reflection)
34. M79-81
35. Mark 15:42-43, M158-159
36. M323-325
37. Abib, also known as Nisan, is the first month of the Hebrew year for festivals. Nisan became the common name for this month after the Babylonian captivity.
38. M162
39. Hebrews 9:11-12
40. 1 Peter 3:18-20
41. M84, (Epstein, The Babylonian Talmud: Seder Mo'ed, 1938), Tractate Shabbath, Chapter IX, 84b-85a.– Note: The original language uses the term "Sabbath eve," rather than Friday – both refer to the sixth day of the week.
42. Deuteronomy 16:1
43. M86 (Three Encampments)
44. Numbers 33:1-8
45. Exodus 14:27-30
46. Leviticus 23:10-11, M94-100
47. M93-94

# Endnotes

48. Colossians 2:16-17
49. 1 Corinthians 15:20, M169
50. 1 Corinthians 15:23
51. 1 Corinthians 15:52 - "In a moment, in the twinkling of an eye, at the last trumpet; for the trumpet will sound, and the dead will be raised imperishable, and we will be changed.", M171
52. M105-106
53. M115
54. Exodus 20:18
55. Exodus 20:22
56. The Feast of Weeks is also called Pentecost, since pentecost is the Greek word for fiftieth... this feast is observed on the fiftieth day after First Fruits.
57. M106-115
58. Deuteronomy 16:3
59. John 7:38-39
60. Acts 2:1-4
61. Acts 1:8
62. Titus 3:5-6
63. Colossians 2:17
64. M189-190 and 348-350
65. M191-193
66. M193-194
67. M194-196
68. M191
69. Revelation 10:7 "...but in the days of the voice of the seventh angel, when he is about to sound, then the mystery of God is finished, as He preached to His servants the prophets."
70. Matthew 24:30-31, M197-198
71. 1 Thessalonians 4:16-17, M206-209
72. 1 Corinthians 15:51-52, M202-205
73. Revelation 11:15, M209-214
74. Matthew 24:42
75. Leviticus 23:27, M217 and M348-350
76. M219 (The Meaning of Atonement)
77. M242 – The Day of Atonement ceremony is described in the 16th chapter of Leviticus.

78. 1 John 2:2 – "And He Himself is the propitiation for our sins; and not for ours only, but also for those of the whole world."
79. M233-234
80. Leviticus 16:2, M235-236
81. Leviticus 16:21-22, M238-240
82. Hebrews 8:5, M222
83. M243
84. M235-236 (A Sinful Man Standing Face-to-Face with the Lord)
85. M242 and M245
86. Hebrews 9:11-12, M245
87. Acts 13:38-39
88. M249-250
89. M250 & 256
90. M252 (A Historical Commemoration)
91. M250
92. 2 Chronicles 5:11-14
93. Revelation 21:1-3
94. Revelation 22:3, M259-262
95. Revelation 22:3-5
96. M276-279
97. M283-284
98. John 14:2-3

# Notes

www.ingramcontent.com/pod-product-compliance
Lightning Source LLC
LaVergne TN
LVHW052311100826
845147LV00006B/729